THIS WALKER BOOK BELONGS TO:

Benjamin

I'm Mam Spamme – terror of the Seven Seas! I'm about to tell you the tale of how we won the treasure of Captain Blood and defeated Red Roger, the wicked Governor of Chutney Island. And to make sure you don't fall asleep while I'm telling it, I'm going to give you puzzles to solve as you go along, so keep your eyes peeled and your wits sharp. First of all, meet the Heroes and Villains.

MAM SPAMME
Me. The Heroine!

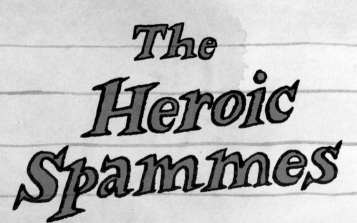

SAM SPAMME
My son. The greediest pirate afloat.

BLACK DOG
The bravest, most intelligent dog in this story.

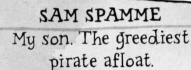

The Heroic Spammes

THE SPOTTED DOG
Our ship.

THE RAT CREW
Brave, reckless and a bit unlucky.

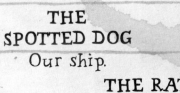

The LOST TREASURE of CAPTAIN BLOOD

How the infamous Spammes escaped the jaws of death and won a vast and glorious fortune.

RED ROGER
The Governor of
Chutney Island.

The Dastardly Villains

NELSON
The cruellest cat
ever to swing a
cutlass.

Written by
JONATHAN STROUD

illustrated by
CATHY GALE

To N. and G. with love.
J.S.

To Granny Cooper,
the original Mam Spamme.
C.G.

First published 1996
by Walker Books Ltd
87 Vauxhall Walk, London SE11 5HJ

This edition published 2006

2 4 6 8 10 9 7 5 3 1

Text © 1996 Jonathan Stroud
Illustrations © 1996 Cathy Gale

The right of Jonathan Stroud and Cathy Gale
to be identified as author and illustrator
respectively of this work has been asserted
by them in accordance with the
Copyright, Designs and Patents Act 1988

This book has been typeset in
Alpha Regular and Beta Regular

Printed in China

All rights reserved

British Library Cataloguing in Publication Data:
a catalogue record for this book is available
from the British Library

ISBN-13: 978-1-84428-767-3
ISBN-10: 1-84428-767-X

www.walkerbooks.co.uk

WALKER BOOKS
AND SUBSIDIARIES
LONDON · BOSTON · SYDNEY · AUCKLAND

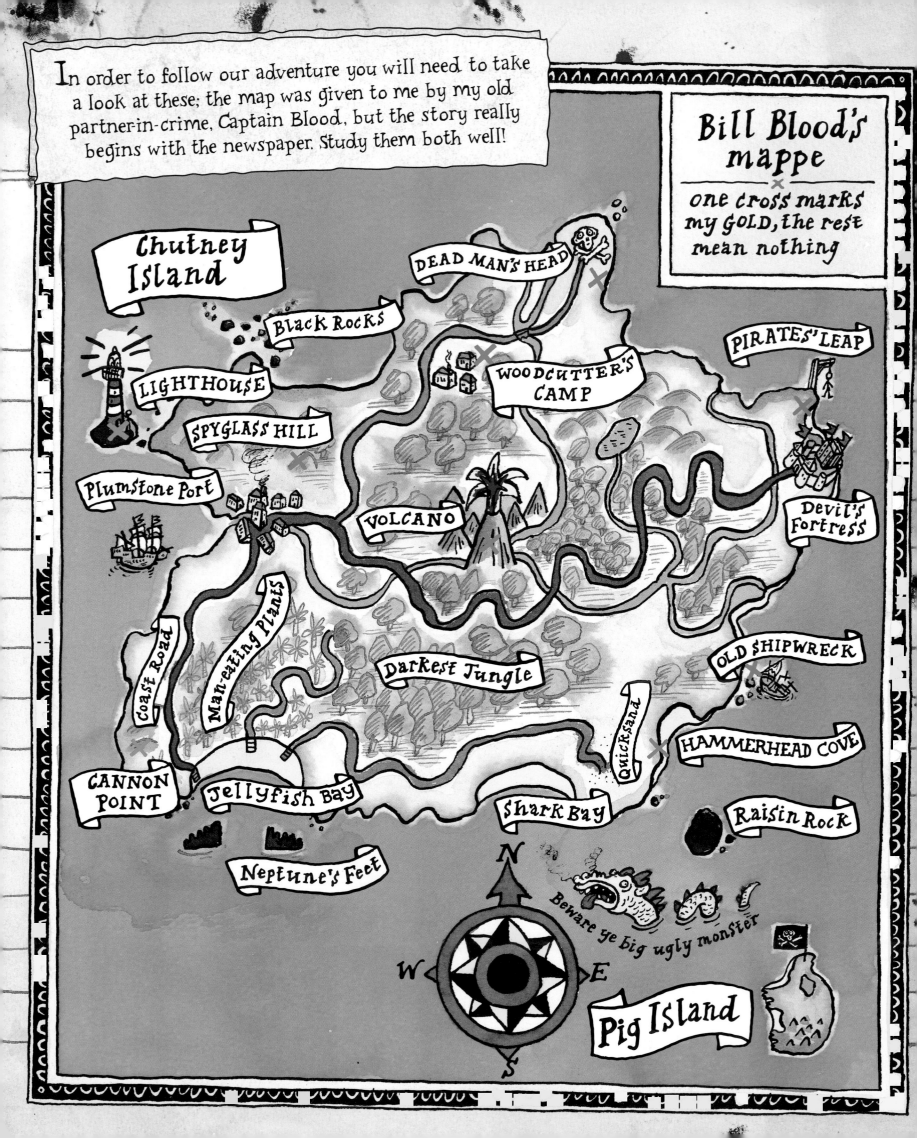

CHUTNEY ARROW

BILL BLOOD CAPTURED!

Bill Blood, the famous pirate, was finally captured last night by our Governor Red Roger and his fearless henchpuss, Nelson the cat. They caught him napping in his cottage on Dead Man's Head and put him in the dungeon of DEVIL'S FORTRESS. He will be taken next week to PIRATES' LEAP and hanged.

TREASURE!

Bill Blood is said to have hidden a huge hoard of treasure somewhere here on CHUTNEY ISLAND. No one knows where it is. He has given his treasure map to his old shipmate, Mam Spamme, for safe-keeping.

Red Roger in Bill Blood's parlour. Blood's belongings were auctioned off this morning.

Fearless henchpuss, Nelson.

ROGER SETS SAIL!

Roger set sail before breakfast, intending to capture his old enemies, the Spammes. He will then use the map to find the treasure and return it to its rightful owners.

Roger's ship, the Semolina.

SPY SETS OUT!

Roger has sent his top spy to follow the Spammes. He will keep well hidden and send messages to Roger using Fred the carrier pigeon.

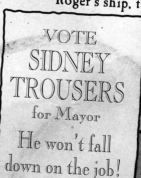

You now have all the information you need to follow the story. Just look out for the puzzles in the black flags and solve them as you go. Now buckle your cutlasses and turn the page.

It was 18th May, 1721. We set sail from Pig Island at dawn, looking for rich merchant ships to rob. Turning left at Raisin Rock, we headed along the coast. Just then, a passing gull delivered a day-old copy of the Chutney Arrow.

Steaming lobsters! Bill's been captured!

R-R-Roger's after us! W-what do we do?

SHIP AHOY!

Is it R-R-ROGER?

It's all right Sam, it's just an old junk.

Hand over your loot!

There's nothing valuable here, ma'am. I got it all dirt cheap at an auction yesterday.

Just then I noticed 4 things belonging to Bill. We had to rescue them. What were they?

Got any grub on board?

No, sir — this is just a junk junk you see.

The sailor was fibbing! Can you find 5 different kinds of food on board?

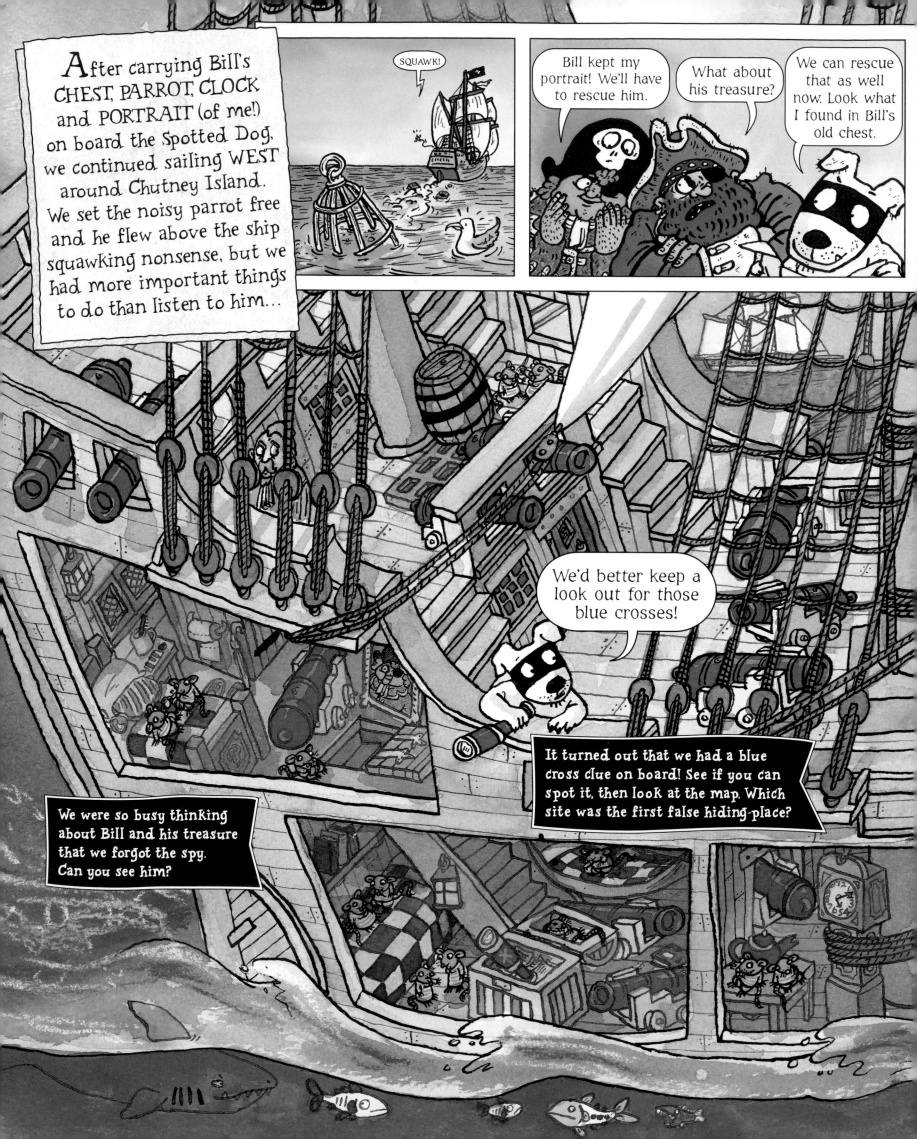

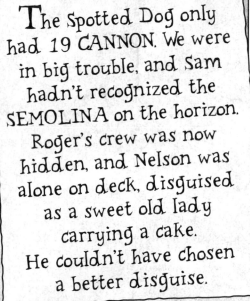

The Spotted Dog only had 19 CANNON. We were in big trouble, and Sam hadn't recognized the SEMOLINA on the horizon. Roger's crew was now hidden, and Nelson was alone on deck, disguised as a sweet old lady carrying a cake. He couldn't have chosen a better disguise.

Cake ahoy! Let's board 'em! I'm starving!

Sam, wait! STOP!

Back — you scurvy molluscs!

I mustn't forget the blue crosses in all this excitement!

Where was the next blue cross?

He hasn't got a wooden leg!

What IS that parrot on about?

One slice of Spamme coming up!

Ulp! I've dropped me cutlass!

The sneaky spy was still nearby. Where was he hiding?

My prawn-brained son was in trouble again! How did he escape from Nelson and get back on board the Spotted Dog?

SEMOLI

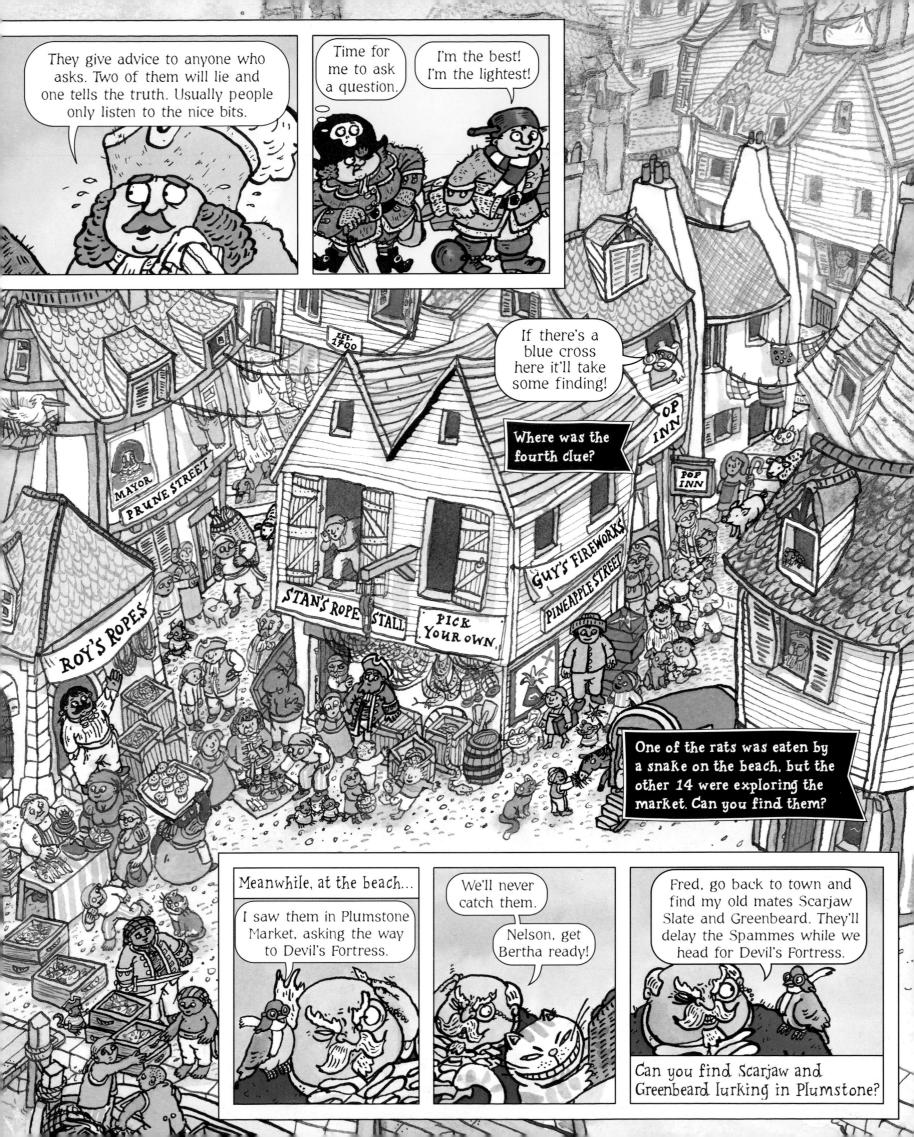

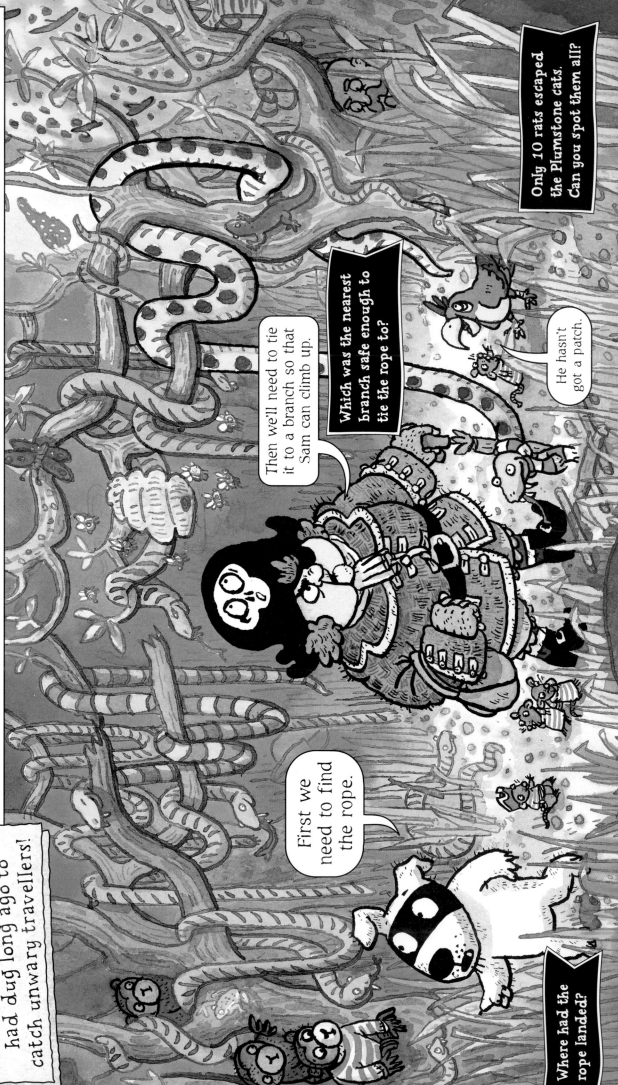

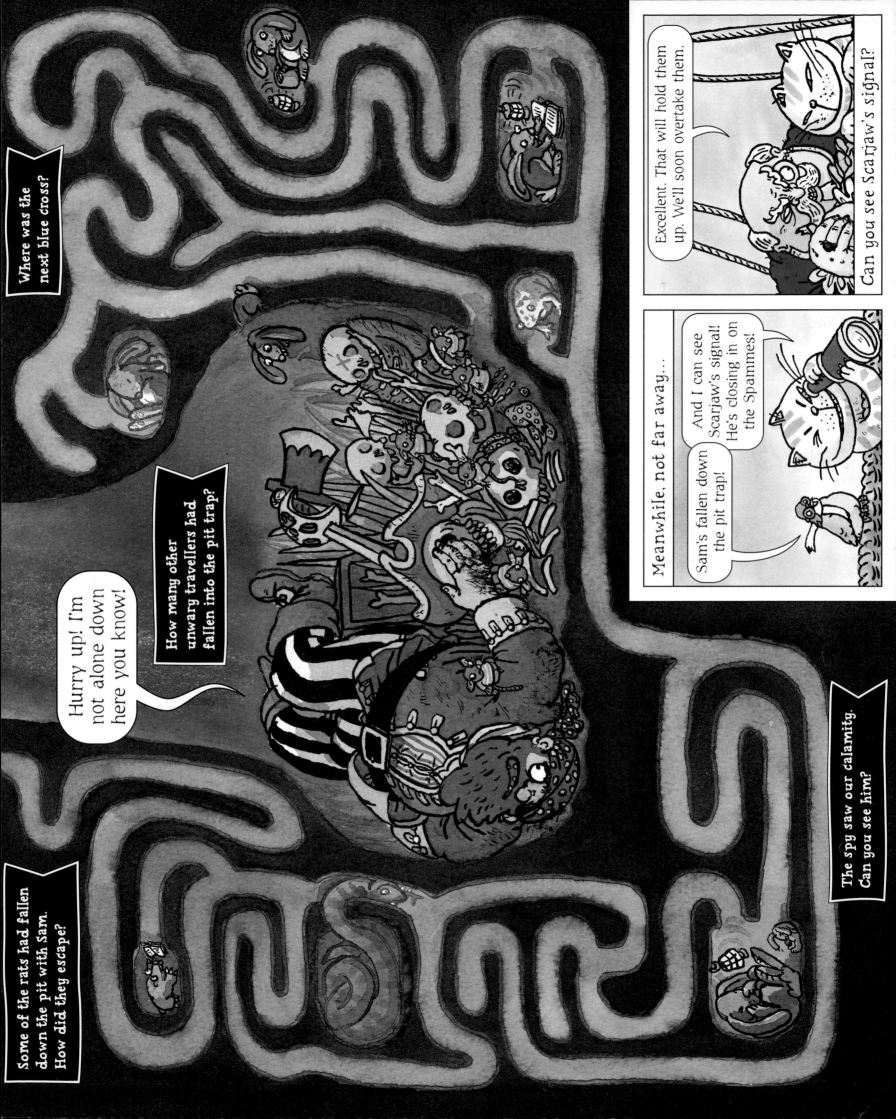

We found the rope in the trees and tied it to the branch with a BUTTERFLY on it. Sam said goodbye to the 5 SKELETONS and climbed out - but our troubles had only just begun! Scarjaw had signalled to Roger with his SPOTTED HANDKERCHIEF and was preparing to attack.

They've escaped the pit! CHARGE!!

Scarjaw! Greenbeard! There are too many! Run for your lives!

Yes, but which way?

Get them!

I'll never overeat again!

Puff!

We were lost in the deepest, darkest bit of jungle, but we escaped by using our wits. Follow each of my JUNGLE SURVIVAL TIPS in turn and work out how we escaped without retracing our steps.

MAM'S JUNGLE SURVIVAL TIPS

1. Cross at the log bridges but beware:

red spruce trunks are rotten - avoid them!

2. Now find some flowers.

3. Take them to the wild bees and exchange them for some honey.

4. Head for the bear - avoid the fire termites...

and the ferocious jaguar.

5. Offer the honey to the bear and slip past.

6. Find the place with 2 boats tied up together. Alligators overturn boats with more than 2 passengers.

7. Float downstream to Devil's Fortress, avoiding all the whirlpools.

Bertha the BALLOON took Roger to the fort in double-quick time. We arrived in a sorry state. Someone had to get us past the guard to rescue Bill, and Sam drew the short straw.

Who goes there?

As if I couldn't guess.

G-good day. Er, we are four pir—er wandering oddjobbers and we are very, very honest and we've never ever been to sea.

May we go inside and do, er, any odd jobs, um, you might be wanting done?

Certainly — you seem an honest fellow.

Idiot!

Thanks to Sam we had to do all the rotten jobs around the fort until we found the dungeon door. Follow our trail from soldier to soldier.

Right, oddjobbers, report to Captain Jones, gatehouse, top floor, silly moustache.

Fix the loose tile in the top turret, then visit Smith in the room two floors below the tile.

Muck out the pigs in the sty please, chaps. Then visit Ogilvy: he's two floors above the sty and two rooms along.

Broken flagpole! Needs mending! Then visit O'Brien: he's hanging out his washing.

The squirrel monkeys had invited 2 of our rats to visit their banana plantation, but there were still 7 left to raid the fort. Can you track them down?

Nelson made his choice...

WHOOPS! Wrong one!

Ha-harr!

CLANG!

Caught in their own trap!

Nothing can stop us n-eh?

MAM!

MAM!

MAM!

Mam, you old walrus!

Mam! Let me out!

Oh, no! They're all so dirty and ugly, any one of them could be Bill!

1 2 3 4 5

6 7 8 9 10

He hasn't got a red hat!

Wait! The parrot knows the answer! He's been telling us all along!

Three rats were raiding the kitchen, but 4 were exploring the dungeon. Can you find them?

The parrot's squawks were not nonsense after all! Look back at all his clues and work out which prisoner was the real Bill Blood. Can you pick out the spy as well?

WAIT! Before you turn over, find the eighth and last blue cross clue! When you've found and solved it, you should have just one possible treasure site left on your map! If you think you know where it is, read on!

Suddenly, everything was going right! If Nelson had cut the rope tied to the YELLOW lever, we would have been flatter than flatfish. But he'd cut the BROWN one and the villains were trapped. While Sam tied them up, the parrot's clues led us straight to CELL 9! I broke the door down and Bill was free! Now we had to escape.

Look what I've found!

TO BEACH

Ooof!

One escape later...

Hurrah! We're out! Now for Bill's treasure!

Clever of you to hide it near the dreaded gallows – the last place any pirate would want to look!

You're right. The chest's in one of those caves...

Trouble is, I can't remember which. And I left deadly spiders in the others. We'll have to use the sum I invented to remind me.

There was nothing for it but to solve Bill's sum. We found the right cave, eventually. Can you?

Even after Roger's capture, his spy couldn't get out of the habit of watching us! Can you spot him?

BILL'S SUM

Take the number of PIRATE BOOTS lying on the beach.

Add the number of CARRION CROWS.

Take away the number of SKULLS scattered on the cliffs.

The answer will be the same as the number of SWORDS outside the TREASURE CAVE.

The wind was blowing OUT TO SEA, and Roger and Nelson soon drifted over the horizon. When the coast was clear, we scrambled up to the cliff face and poked around inside the cave with 3 SWORDS - the left nostril. Rich pickings indeed!

At last, we saw our reward!

We carried our loot back to Plumstone Port...

We never did work out what happened to the spy. Perhaps we left him behind on Chutney Island. What do you think?

This is the life! Good food...

Good company!

The new crew soon spotted Sam's big appetite! Can you find 9 scattered banana skins on deck?

...and there's even good weather too!

Two rats got lost on the cliffs, so only one member of our rat crew made it on board the Spotted Dog II. Can you see him? Why wasn't he lonely for long?

WALKER BOOKS is the world's leading
independent publisher of children's books.
Working with the best authors and illustrators
we create books for all ages, from babies
to teenagers – books your child will
grow up with and always remember. So…

FOR THE BEST CHILDREN'S BOOKS,
LOOK FOR THE BEAR